A Biography in Verse

Elliott

A Biography in Verse

A Poem by

Jason David Peterson

Distillate Press
Minneapolis, MN

Published by Distillate Press
Copyright © 2015 by Jason David Peterson
All rights reserved
FIRST PRINTING

TYPEFACE: Calibri/Leelawadee

Acknowledgement is made to members of the Saint Paul Poetry Workshop for their review and support throughout the making of this book.

ISBN-13: 978-0692473825
ISBN-10: 0692473823

Contents

E1. 1

    Elliott found 3
    We talk of webs 4
    When Elliott is out 5
    Elliott's youth is 6
    An old playground 7
    House centipede 8
    The piano barks 9
    A drink to Elliott 10
    From sink to self 11
    Nine weeks 12
    Leaning in mirror 13
    When Elliott eats 14
    A reticent whorl 15
    His remaining 16

E2. 17

    New things catch 19
    Believe oneself 20
    All you'd expect 21
    An afternoon 22
    A tool applied 23
    Having pulled 24
    It's a mistake 25
    Through time 26
    He never found 27

E3. 29

    Elliott is 31
    Head-caged 32
    Back to work 33
    He strikes 34
    Of art and 35
    Birdsong 36
    Click fuzz 37

- ELLIOTT'S SPEECH IS 38
- A VAST MINING VESSEL 39
- BURDENFEET 40
- HE KNOWS LABOR 41
- SWOLLEN WITH HIM 42
- UNDERGONE 43

E4. 45

- FIRST CRUMBS 47
- ELLIOTT SETS HIS OWN 48
- IT'S A HELL OF A THING 49
- MEASURE THE SPACE 50
- THE MONEY COMES 51
- THERE'S A SEA 52
- UNHINGED 53
- WHAT IS 54
- ELLIOTT'S SPACE 55

E5. 57

- HE TELLS OF 59
- THE BIND 60
- THE HEAT POOLS 61
- THROUGH TOWN AND 62
- WHAT IS ELLIOTT WHEN 63
- HE MOVES BETWEEN 64

LETTERS TO ELLIOTT 65

- IN HER EYES, YOU STAND 67
- ELLIOTT, THERE IS A NAME 68
- ELLIOTT, WHY IS IT? 69
- I'VE WATCHED MY HAND 70
- I'VE SEEN A TIRED ELLIOTT 71
- YOU WERE IN MY DREAM 72
- YOU WERE WRONG 73
- SOMETIMES 74

NOTES 75

What are the roots that clutch, what branches grow
Out of this stony rubbish? Son of man,
You cannot say, or guess, for you know only
A heap of broken images...

—T.S. Eliot, *The Waste Land*

e1.

INTERPHASE

#1

Elliott found a lie in his yard
slow-motion hammering
up through the tar of the driveway;
another, creeping out from under
the tall pine fence of his neighbor;
a fine sliver of lie, wheeling down
a thin logic line from a deep
breath-held sky. He summoned
his boyhood, a brute training
in truth, and began to consume
—arrived the wild eater of lies.
Now his yard is pocked and his sky
is marred, a full city-lot of scars,
and Elliott's kin must decide
of him, self-bitten and bulged,
if he's looking more a hero
of war, or sadly, simply deformed.

#2

We talk of webs
like metaphors are
unalterably anchored
in tradition, sometimes
fateful tines spun
as from puppeteers,
or net-traps catching us
in florid misdirection.
Elliott bores of this,
spreads oar and pulls
the rope in—his web
is a map of facts
and all their sordid
quixotic relations,
a reference for his
existential location.
Fiction, on the other hand
is nurtured likewise
in the abdomen,
but let loose in
more wasp-like fashion
—a part of himself
is lost upon injection.

#3

When Elliott is out of alignment
the pain can be a thumbpress
or a gravity sledge, pounding
new orbits. Even positrons
are known to coalesce
along a trap axis—
perhaps it's unavoidable
he plucks the pen and drools
long trails of nothing.
Like the quantum leap,
the unreal it seems
is ever brimming
to pass that pinnacle
and burst into being.
There's a fear Elliott
is the opposite,
perpetually aiming
to decomposit.

#4

Elliott's youth is a bank of sand,
tenacious march, pole-foot
and rake-hand to the king's perch
then uncrowned and reversed.
His sun-fed impetuous arms
drive cool into the hillside,
all bird-holed, grubbed
and snake-eyed—sometimes
something awaits hidden
and horror-laced and skin
remembers, pressure-chest
and quiver, we mustn't dig.
Other times there is only hole.
And years later, the bank
hauled off to level basements
and fill swamps, his heart
strains back-fired and mulling
—a rediscovery of that dark,
damp fistful of nothing.

#5

An old playground
bent of storm, ploughed
of stance, carved
and tagged and culled
to scrap by the cult
of indifference—
looking on, lost
Elliott is a memory trust
with no beneficiary,
a sentimental liability,
a childhood held up by sand
—fear in a handful of rust.
He walks the shrapnel garden
head-hung for the hyacinths,
prunes a bald spike
with a bicycle chain,
buries his hope like the bulb
and secretly remains.

#6

House centipede
in the dim and hymnal
quiet of the evening
assumes exilious privacy,
zips and scutters
like a loosed pen
in a drunk philanthropy,
but Elliott is attuned—
bee-lines the rag
and hand broom;
the narcoleptic hunt
resumes, and terror
sharp and embarrassed,
not by the bug or bite
but the way the thing moves:
a foreign, jittery train
of legs and segments
unnervingly smooth.
He has to end it,
recalibrate the known
physics of motion—
the clean pine floor
waxed and yellowed
shines empty,
an emptiness shone.

#7

The piano barks and coos
its long anacrusis,
the sound of wilderness
in the key of duress
sustained by an ale,
a muddy red drain
down a pipe of throat,
and everything
about Elliott
is a half-note—
the daily refrain
of dreams and doubts,
his muttered placido
in a canon of house,
the way light
decrescendos
from a bronze daylamp
to the worn pockets
of the past—
such withdrawal
is a mar in life's melody.
Played Elliott is focused
and torn; a measure of scars
in a slowly muting discord.

#8

A drink to Elliott
is an honor not for praise
or commissary, not even
the loose blood
of a shared history,
but a flowing nod
to volition—
one is set upon
and expended,
the other partakes
and is poisoned
with life—what
metabolic violence!
He is a byproduct
of the tiny war
yet guides it.
Every pour
a secret arming
of the evening's
wine regime,
another gastric
cannibal trap—
chemical spoils seized.
Elliott is pure profit
and something dark
is feeding off it.

#9

From sink to self
in sickness thick
it formalized.
Not the contents
of the stomach
so much the mojo
of its image, he spewed
a half-choked surprise
and paused.
What the body urges,
nothing comes—
and isn't that the prize
of cerebral miners?
To be true to himself
is division, Elliott's
anti-urgent intuition
and his ornate appetites.
Now that there's another,
who will wear the mouth
of the other?

#10

Nine weeks quarantined
like old leftovers in the pot,
a sealed-up bodyslosh;
no full-spectrum Elliott
but an afterswatch—
one the artist might use
when the sun is diffused
and all records of pattern
go lost in the hurricane
of microbial bedlam.
Faintly confused, the
baked mud of sickness
vaults him like currency
—useless at rest
and of little interest,
but see what happens
when he outlasts. Elliott's
health is a gamble
that broken of spirit
the spirit has value.

#11

Leaning in mirror, he trips
on the frame of himself
and siderolls into fracture
—his purview accessed
from each peripheral
screams a pang
of connection; every
little slivered him,
a smatter of ants
on the honey trail
of mortality—
restless, hungry,
infectiously embodied.
The trails meander
climbing out from under
pools of oil, veins of gold,
sweat, lipstick, everything
honey-wet and pliant,
then the trophied return
to the nest—and there again
is Elliott, piecing together
and pacing for the onset
of the something greater.

#12

When Elliott eats
it's not to fill his gut
but to conquer the world
internally, chemically,
piece by piece, like that man
who ate an airplane
though more subtly.
Each digestive passing
a stroke of the ego,
a mark of his existence
left organically. That way,
if upon death there's no
holy father to impress
with his collective moral deeds,
at least the microbes will remember
and spin with awe at the evidence
of something larger than belief.

#13

A reticent whorl of thoughtmeal
took Elliott from his robe and slump,
pressed him to the hand-gummed glass
and set his jaw ticking to the beat
of the midday clap—outside a nut falls
from the packed mouth of a chipmunk,
a crushed can rattles a jettison path
from the arm-cave of a passing sedan,
the dancing phone lines swing a jig
of wiretap on the tar-bled roofs
of sun-bathed homes and sheds
—there is a world around his sphere
of dramatic stillness, a way to move
without swathing the motion
in a cocoon of analysis,
and Elliott is a bath of static
buzzing with the action of atoms
telling him to break, to build and burn,
come apart and only partially return.

#14

His remaining indoors
was consent, a low bow
to a sturdy frame
of encumbrance,
like a second shadow.
As Elliott goes
hesitant steps
brave him out
to a wider structure
—a blinding
infinite blueprint
thick of lines
that turn on his will
with the torque
of horizons, until
the black behind him
an optic pinhole
—a brilliant theft
of displacement
so that everything
current is present,
even the gone who
wrap him in absence
—such a unity to suffer
and maybe that's home:
not the stronghold
of concord and hope,
but a world of things
we'd never have made
if all who left had stayed.

e2.

PROPHASE

#15

New things catch him
by misdirection—when plans
upturn, foundations keeling,
play goes paramount,
head-walks the ceiling
—stairwells grow cliffs,
cupboards to crawlspace
and all the escapes
now doughty lunges
in the strung frontiers of fate.
Though why the shake?
What pinch awakes
lax Elliott—the attention
he's paid in full, the likes
which rarely dull
and drift as leaves
from glance to blow
but step like hooves
about the heart,
pounding a hard-line
overdose of life
—damn the risk
and why. Survival
is one of two genuine crimes.
He could blame the stars
but they've many alibis,
so then commit the other:
when his number's drawn
he'll not take cover.

#16

Believe oneself glass and all
bright inside will pass through,
allowing such blue-hued fragility
to reconstitute the nerve,
routing others, save the perverse
or dysfunctionally wooed—
both of who are present
in this bawdy measurement
of man—Elliott
is a tottery kickstand
for the double-parked soul
that leans timorously
near her window. Smash
is the alarm they've both set.
One man's kindness
is another's epithet.

#17

All you'd expect
from a communion
of neglect—indulgence
in the basics, then
the upward maslow crawl
until a twist of neck
acknowledges
the depth of the fall.
She was linear too
but crossed Elliott
on a different axis,
and as they grew
so did the unseen
dimension in-between.
Elliott is a tangent
romanticized, and
once a line is drawn,
what's a line to do?

#18

An afternoon dry of sound,
burnt of leaves, the sun's
shroud covering a city—
thick drapes of light
starving all disguise
—Elliott and the hound
lock eyes and tremble.
Its snout the long of desire,
nostrils fluted for the hint,
stiff-tailed and testing
it follows the flint of him—
from rat's tooth to the hackles
of the Earth, the threat
is in the temperament,
but untempered Elliott
lives a gap, fills
with the low fog
of war—eventually
a signal will flash,
forcing a clash of will
and he must discover
his howl, or back down
his own black alley of jowls.

#19

A tool applied without restraint
to pry the sinewy splines
and muscled plates, to break
into the gnarled hard-shell
walnut of panic and need
that pushes bravery
through the brigade
of a war-torn self-efficacy
—the blunt puncture
of a love in full remission
leaves a tender Elliott
swimming indecision: to cap
the breach and crystallize
from the wait of it, or oblate
to ruptured splendor
and deflation, in a lengthwise
stumbling grab at salvation.

#20

Having pulled the dead root
that won't shake, only
to drag loose behind him
and swell at the outtake,
she is the tooth unreadied
for the yank, and Elliott
for lack of doorknobs
hobbles from his head,
curdling in the unsaid.
What is this living test
of resilience—
a two-stamened bloom
that eats its own pollen,
a swollen moon that pales
for no one, a harvest year
in a life unchosen—how
in all the grace of time
can one suck out the passion
with the same fangs
that placed it? When
is a wasted thing wasted?

#21

It's a mistake to apply love
like a salve in the wound of
another's heart, if you intend
to escape the mending—
a living glue of platelets and
unending pull will keep you
past the point of virtue,
where only fervent twists
and dissonance can loose
those taut black straps
of unrequitedness. Elliott
makes a list of repairs,
examining the mess
but knows not yet
if it's his or theirs.

#22

Through time
the frost root burrows
in pocks and cracks,
the costume of Elliott
glazed in the windsplash
of a closeness, idealized
from a distance,
unhad—just prints
of half-iced hands
once held forcefully
loose, their oils
keeping even now
a full freeze incomplete
—these are the bones
picked in whispers,
the siren song
of life's winding murmur,
the lockless door
whose muffled knock
he might answer
if known himself caged.

#23

He never found it—
that thing of all chase,
the pit floor, the space
on the other side of the door
—but Elliott bores of hunger.
He's discovered something
more complete: a cherishing
of gap, a humble honoring
of the fragile carafe
of his body as it always
and with marked progress
proceeds to defront
and deliquesce,
pool as nutrients
—make more room
for the mournful appetite
of the rest to bloom.

e3.

METAPHASE

#24

Elliott is on the moon,
the dark and empty blue
hues blanket the planes
of his room—what full
light does serenely
diffused in dust,
a kind of canvas
to ink and brand
with the phantoms
of imagination.
Shadow lines liven
to a count, four mouths
cardinal calling
for the reroute—a reason
to step out or linger,
three measured hands
closing up to capture
his imperfect framework,
bronze him in it
like a shrine to recognition
—a desire of the living
to goad him into relevance,
a negative of the world's lust
for meaning, but Elliott
knows he is only
a switch of a circuit
in the essence machine
with one way in
and two ways out:
die and somehow live
or die and die, unshow
and untell—a practice
for the shadows
to learn about themselves.

#25

Head-caged Elliott
demotes the pen
—to the source
his arms bend, intern
on hair and skin,
holding the skull
as a cauldron,
a shook bottle
or rattle bomb
of ambition,
a steam chamber
of gripe and grammar
piping to blow
in a pin-fury
of expression so
inflated with farce
and wound in obtuse
clairvoyance
that futures wince
and tremble
at the end-state
of conscious potential.
Yet, the narrowing
rut of essentials
drags through him
a linear calm—
his being imagined
without full equation:
the full force
of imagination.

#26

Back to work, held breath
of cares, back down the stairs,
legs carried faster than air
by tidal forces in the great
pitch of space (still relatively
immobile), but no one takes
the time to analyze a trifle
of descending inconsistency;
a man drops eleven feet
without flexing anything
but the bitterslow pinch
of begrudging redundancy
—just floats down inanely.
It's not his narrowed aim
or a social imperative,
but a way to contain
derivatives, so that life
is withheld to the inch
to be leeched out slowly,
discreetly, onanisticly.
A small ration of security
in an infant world with no mother.
A limping courage on the crutch
of a feckless, anomic none-other.

#27

He strikes the Enter key,
extends the program
from its housing
into false bodies
of silicon and wire,
so Elliott is abandoned
of onus, while
the code of him
rewrites the world
in little, irreversible ways.
Someday the recordings
of a self reduced
to storage will play
and its vacant timbre
will awaken in him
the default settings
of a species—
the simple binary
of take or leave,
and he'll know
if such will
was ever free.

#28

Of art and culture
and mimicry, Elliott inquires
of the TV and it listens
slug-mouthed and riotous,
ready to save us at the cost
of pulling from the road
a generation of broken
and propping it on the love
that pain has for itself.
His asking irrelevant
—there is no screen,
only a feign of distance
between subject and object,
a line whose own line has drawn
and faded, yet one after another
retraces to ensure the glass
of the microscope won't crack
against the anodized tragic of the slide.
Elliott has so much to unask,
such foaming mystery to rebottle
in flesh and slowly detox of it.
The answers might enlighten,
to what truth—that answers exist,
and an average of apathy.
That the average becomes truth,
having then no use of it.
That Elliott must be made to lie
in the street, under a wreck of truth,
and cry out for the saving pull of teeth.
That the television is breathing, stilled,
dug in for the pounce, and the rescue.

#29

Birdsong flood of sound,
a sweet lute whine,
dragging drunken whistle
dropped of pitch, a loud
horn cackle, brassy knock
and low earhog pound
scrape and penetrate
—Elliott is torn down
and scattered, made room
for the path of music.
It is beautiful
like in commercials
loosely imagined for him.
Their scripts a fluttered blur
bolstering the vision,
a stampede of look-at-me
and listen. Elliott is invested
in language, and bankrupt
—the sounds
of the throat and mouth
have leveraged meaning
for momentum, and oh
how they've ploughed.

#30

Click fuzz, bold unbending blank,
a power to disengage available
to anyone in reach—it's how
to get by without getting
as by hangs its optimism
on city clothes lines
and lays out for the long drunk,
or as one Elliott turns to a greeting
mistaken, apologetic—as if
participation, accidental even,
is a breach of policy,
as if a message
can secure its relevance
in the halls of heterogeneity.
Another Elliott fails to kowtow
so narratively, pretends
to be the beckoned,
to force the unblanking
and is read for a moment
like every story told
simultaneously—it isn't
it won't and it doesn't,
but somewhere
in the impression
pools clarity.

#31

Elliott's speech is a weave
of incongruent fabrics,
as mixed metaphors are
extensively more accurate
than a fixed description
of a thing at its reach.
The world, for instance,
is a tethered tumbleweed
of indifference, in a space-box
where each conscious slough
of instinct is of vital importance
—like a divine painter resigned
to minimalist caricature,
or a landscaper eloped
to a life of love at sea—these
are not the one-in-a-millions
but the hijacked majority
of cultured cavemen, wandering
the ethics of existence
and the Chinese finger-traps
of their own bodies. Elliott's
mess is equally significant;
a tangle in the mesh
of collective experience.

#32

A vast mining vessel envelopes
a planet Elliott dreams, backlit
by the unfathomable mind slate.
His new-age fears arise in forms
of technological rampage, unchecked
governments, financial slave trade
—his scuttling eyes sink and vein,
logging red hours in volumes
and databanks, exposing conspiracy
maybe, but unconsciously seeking
a warm hand to stop-hold calm
and pluck away the tight-wound strings
of supersociety from his shoulders,
show him a world where honest work
is more than a sharehold of extortion,
that the name of a color is unequivocal
to its shade and hue, that a healthy soul
cannot survive the clench of debt
—though some days, clouded in
and labeled blue, he'd settle
for a hand to wipe the sweat.

#33

Burdenfeet, socks drawn
like ankled dew rags,
loafers squeezed over
the hook-toed bloat of damp
and hammered callous,
his aching joints
in rocking motion pull
what life resides
exiguous in the skin
of the earth, painfully
through the floor,
forcing it up the legs
each morning—keeping
this body, too calmed
with stale intolerance
and worn of living,
from folding back
in a stone-roll of apathy.
Elliott is a temple, barely.
We see the pillars
no man can enter,
the time-weathered promise
half buried in irrelevance,
the unsummoned glory
of existence soured
in the sweat of the ordinary;
He's an argument
for the arch of story,
as heavenly, as
sound as any.

#34

He knows labor
like years laid
between great wars;
a celebration at first,
free from toil, the
deserved half-work
of screens and service,
then the roll of roles
and a nervous slide
to atrophy—a recall,
the true strain of ease:
defined by deeds,
with nothing done and
a waning smoke's shadow
of ability, a raw thirst
for gruel and sweat
overwhelms—unquenched
in the long lax, Elliott
watches for the chance
at friction and impact
to wake the body,
make a pain exact,
reinsert the gear of him
in the mortal machine
—give the end a means
it can't forget.

#35

Swollen with him
the rule bulges,
yaws and spills
open. He is free of it
like a moment broken
from an image
and growing
by the minute.
But it wasn't time
or any specific limit
that drew him in
to drown—Elliott
had expected so,
and each of those
collected more
of the rule around him.
What lost its effect,
which allowed
the decampment,
was death—acceptance
has robbed it of its threat.

#36

Undergone a small melt,
his brain buckle burst,
numbers fell away
from their host thoughts
like moons of retired orbits
—the facts of him
left dim in the haze
of mindspace. Then
a crescendo of hope,
chemical and guttural
—with precision exposed
as spiritual biopsy,
the limitlessness
stretched a morning yawn,
quietly wrapping itself
in Elliott, and moving on.

e4.

ANAPHASE

#37

First crumbs of winter tumble,
dander on the air, tickle
the troposphere—then
the heavy northern sneeze
that leaves us wet and wind-burned
yet marching for the tempered rush
of survival—because there's nothing
in our boots to harden the path,
no terror in the television real enough
to say "breathe, or the lungs will cease."
So that ten minute walk from the bus stop
is Elliott's hour, sleet-soaked socks
and snow down his collar, bent low
and trudging humble to kick the coals,
stir up those floundering ashes
of the ever-summer-soul
then finally home, hands
on the window—yes there's life
in the warm hole of the sofa,
but his love like a bad dog
is fed and briefly pet in the cold.

#38

Elliott sets his own
balancing on the floor.
"My place is over there
and this is yours." Never
can it fall without spoil, so
he moves around the house,
the world with careful effort
allocating weight to bow
everything in cohort
and keep it poised. He knows
his patterned end—
won't own his own again,
bares his scar undressed in
complete repletion, bellows
a fair-shared tocsin, and
keeps his globe-eyes open
for a warm hearted tailor
with no impulse to cover
his condition. Elliott
is a debt to himself,
half forgiven.

#39

It's a hell of a thing
that can take the color
out of a girl's hair
just by staring,
or bring down satellites
with a reckless yawn
—that daunting sun
beyond the airs.
Elliott's yawns
wouldn't startle cats
but oh, how his stares
have sought more than color.
Sometimes he dreams,
hot summer sleep, to be made
in that flaming image;
to flash and fray in the void,
burning through to satisfy
the hunger, to wake up
in a sweat, cold black density,
unseen in the contrast of shadows.

#40

Measure the space, near
light years between faces
—he could muster such
a skin-tucked smile,
and by the time it struck
her eyes he may have walked
another life, wondering
if the amorous look
he swallowed hard
was just a flickering
shape in the gas-lit cloud
of eternity, or was she only
fumbling sloppy glee
from a half-lost bird song
in a childhood memory?
He does a fair loon call,
and either way an echo
forms eventually—
like the upturned lip
of humanity bored
with sorrow and finally
searching—even darkness
calls on eyes to know it,
and of the silence, gas-lit
Elliott smiles tenderly,
earfully, for nobody.

#41

The money comes
in *fun size*, mislabeled
agony of a brief taste
and pocket of appetite
—Elliott is green with debt,
a full orchestra of nausea:
from the course jangle
of coin-counted rent,
the plucked strings
of spent savings, a slow
trumpet drain of interest,
to the sharp ring
of collection calls
and hollow jug blow
of his bank accounts
—the distinct value
of an Elliott life and
all that might matter
to another. But then
she grabs his aging hand,
and somewhere out there
the anomaly is quantified,
a fee is paid.

#42

There's a sea between Elliott
and the pure of his dreams,
a watery hill of green
carrying the ghost call
of accord, tired and shorn
with compromise, off
at a constant rise—
his numb, fumbling paddle
is a play on enterprise
when the towline of hope
snap-severs from tangle
in a need-bogged weed bed.
What can be said of the throw
and chase, the soaking
pattern of displacement,
the breathing of water
so regular the burn changes
species—what becomes Elliott
if not altered completely?

#43

Unhinged by an ageless intimacy,
he throws a dark arm in the mis-
angled cupboards of strangeness,
feeling for the ridge of things
—what shapes can be named
in attraction when the body
is a means to empathy, and fetish
the curt-adolescence of exploration?
Elliott finds such open spaces,
in the seamless carpentry
of relations, inviting—
as for the building inspectors
(all scoff and measure), discretion's
his reluctant meed, and yet
what language swells from within
like sap, so sweet in its subtlety.

#44

What is a shared space, mulls
aging Elliott, full bare—the brunt
of venned boundaries paired
with a styed eye for gender
psychology. Is there a way
to vinegar the sinuses
of masculine routine,
silence that proud refrain
of self-sufficiency our
ancestors played on repeat
through every faultless bout
of dependency, and wake up
a warm-eared stranger
in the concert of another's
company? Or is the age-
old recipe of disconnect and
stumbling hierarchy, the sway
of impulse and hot conceit,
his only option—to mystify
the attraction and let breathe
such suffocating caution.

#45

Elliott's space is vital,
an intimate absence
that carries more in it
than the breadth of clutter,
but these others invited
become the space,
their names hang on it,
a choking of names
in the throat of creation
—his courtship with
the unmade, unmade
as all discovered, prized
and tamed stifle ambition,
foretell decision, divert
the I in long servitude
of we; this is the end
of bold and boastful misery,
the beginning of someone
more or less complete.

e5.

TELOPHASE

#46

He tells of a nail in a paint-chipped
and faded wood—the routine
of slamming something heavy
across its piled head until it sinks
with cork-like reluctance
in a small round house of rejection.
So much depends on the mating
of these elements, the truss
and the rafter, the rust and
the rapture, that heavy hearts
which pull by their weights apart
have no future in grip or ground
—they suspend in a cycle
of hammered attempts,
and somehow Elliott
honors the sadness
in every swing, and it echoes
the love we have
for all things old.

#47

The bind of ambiguity
allows a world of things
to feign as family—
indefinite Elliott
has many relatives
he's never seen.
As how not to love
one flavor or another
makes a sterile tongue,
his open arms
have wrung him
something vital.
Elliott dares himself
to action—to find
and reignite his passion.

#48

The heat pools like rain in stark
patch lines of tar, the tug and strain
of seams—there's the means
for all manners of change:
the worth of a splint, the fate
of nails, the sway and shape
of continents, the gravity drain
in the overlap of the universe,
even the bleed of a stain—
a tumultuous warfront
on the battlefield of texture.
Live-walking mind-bodies
flood around Elliott, a blunt flow
of friction. Where are the joints
of perspective, the knuckles of flux
where one man's understanding
is another's extension?
Each step in the world a walk
well-balanced on the tar line,
held upright by an infinite
exigent fight.

#49

Through town and wild
Elliott makes himself a whim,
allows the pull and knock
of a country to abuse him
—in part to steal of it
the shape of the wound,
as well to seat a need
he might aspire to:
a northern lake
is poisoned of oil;
a couple marries
on a sun-brushed isle
in the foreshadow of cancer;
and everywhere
a back-page of news
of nations across oceans
falling to ruin—so much
is churned back
into the sludge of birth
that Elliott can't tell
what's more difficile—
to undo or improve,
or whether it's him
or the world
in need of renewal.

#50

What is Elliott when all
that's shot from mouths
are snares of preemption,
wild throws of category,
a forcing of exposition
on misfit sympathies?
Even the question
when level-held
in the cup of him
serves a floor of spill
and quenches only
the mirrored ear.
Here, the effect
is the best definition
—what else can we call
a recurring dream,
or the morality
of an awl, the only
song now playing
in an endless track-list?
Elliott listens too,
thumb-drumming along
and swaying to the great
distance from self,
the greater closeness.

#51

He moves between buildings
like a divergent current
in a city already drowned
in its own progress
—each window drawn
a private show of lung-burn
or the slow float of a burden
let go. The city-center
a relentless fount of pressure
forcing space to spaces,
room to rooms, smoke
and air to glass, grass
to pitch and tar, and Elliott
to age and form—a product
of time in the mill of material.
His hands are not his own,
piled and pulled
and baked and blown,
and every instance of him
driven to its end
like the sand and swill
run toward the drain.
There is a cleanliness,
a matter-of-factness
and yet a chance
like all beginnings have.

Letters to Elliott

CYTOKINESIS

11.

*In her eyes, you stand
like the city's once
proudest sky scraper
fully vacant—the glory
and sway homeless
in the streets around it.
Your unkept frame
reduced to windbreak
and a length of black
on the path behind.
You've been condemned
my poor Elliott. I see it.
A man cannot sustain
the loss of his tenant.*

12.

*Elliott, there is a name
for what your mouth
has broken over.
There are little strings
that go from here
to you, the one buried
beneath the willow,
the forest yet to flow.
Once plucked, each becomes
a song whose notes meander
to the beat of whoever
applies the most pressure.
That nerve you've worn
as a sigil—a struggle
against resonance.
Put down your spool,
your pitch-pipe and mute,
let the losing wake you.*

13.

Elliott, why is it?
Why do you avoid me?
You paper the walls
of your morality with calm
and wholesome patterns
while weathers of desire
billow down, mocking
the muffled rouse of your loins
—you furrow and slaw
at the pull of hair, the
public eye, the unclean
contours of the night, until
there's no secret left to out
—paused in the afterfoam
of your own low-hung mouth.

14.

I've watched my hand
swim across the counter
like a water snake,
quietly and of itself,
feel a book of matches
with amoral curiosity,
like the first time
ever held was a power
to change landscapes.
The same hand that lifts
a glass to me, that pulls
a razor daily, the same
that steers me home
while neglected feet
consider the pedals,
of leaving a mark
of their own.

15.

*I've seen a tired Elliott
tune in the premoment
—the frantic public,
uninterpreted subjects,
disappearing in the grimace.
Here is the way out:
a frame of face, a select action,
a long stare across and we forgive
the ones who bottle handshakes
in a dim room, overdubbed
in contradiction. Look how,
left to imagination, you
let the script of yourself
bloated with pathos, flower out
as soon as you believe.
And we enter you, villains
of allotment—as it seems
what you've done a rare flash.*

16.

You were in my dream.
A panther in the shelf
of a rock-face. A panic
compressing the air.
I saw you in the distance
combing the hillside
with a split branch.
Oblivious I said of you.
Oblivious you said of me.

17.

*You were wrong, Elliott.
There was no greater despair
to wrap in, no comfort
in the space of inaction.
All I discovered in listening
—beneath the layers
of hunger and noise
and the lure of intimacy
—a silence, almost sentient,
searching, listening back at me.*

18.

*Sometimes I'm standing still
looking straight ahead,
thinking but a fraction
of anything, and the sky opens.
Not with space or the cool
palpable dust of eternity,
but the Overwhelming,
the very thing holding
our lives up, keeping them
from blinking out entirely
and it's like all of time is just
this one fragile ornament
that could shatter, sharply
at any moment, if you and I
from opposite sides
were to witness it together.*

Notes

APPENDIX

Chapter banners: Chapters follow the phases of cell division. This strict "bio-graphy" can be read as the division of self that initializes the instant two entities begin to affect or react to one another. In this replication process, no substance is necessarily lost, rather the essence of each entity is spread to others—in a relative sense—through the knowledge and awareness of their being, changing the very composition of self. By extension (perspectives aside), the more two entities interact regularly in an environment of mutual isolation, the more equivalent their composition becomes.

#3: Naturally available energy of positrons can be equalized along the axis of a laser-cooled Penning trap, to form a Coulomb "crystal" of balanced forces. This state is remarkable in that it immobilizes without diminishing impetus. It also sets a moral stage regarding how such trapped energy will be used.

#5: "Fear in a handful of rust" is a play on a line from T.S. Eliot's *The Waste Land*—"I will show you fear in a handful of dust" (30). Hyacinth symbolism is also borrowed here.

#12: In 1980, Michel Lotito (a.k.a. "Mister Eats All") completed his digestion of an entire Cessna 150 airplane. It took him two years to work his way through nearly 1,000 lbs. of minced metal.

#17: "Maslow crawl" refers to developmental psychologist Abraham Maslow's theory of human motivation; i.e. crawling up the de facto pyramid.

#22: The second half of the poem draws on work from multiple authors whose combined subjects form a navigable corridor for accessing a particular, perhaps universal cognitive abyss—the self-made prison. The "bones picked in whispers" refers to T.S. Eliot's *The Waste Land*—"A current under sea / Picked his bones in whispers" (315-316). "Siren song" refers to the musical lure of condemning gratification in Homer's *Odyssey*. "Life's winding murmur" refers to Matthew Arnold's "The Buried Life"—"A man becomes aware of his life's flow, / And hears its winding murmur" (88-89). The "lockless door" refers to Robert Frost's poem of the same name.

#23: "Gap" refers to Jacques Lacan's *objet petit a*, arguably described as the unattainable object cause of desire.

#25: Tension here is best considered under a Nietzschean lens, as demonstrated in his discussion of teaching in *The Wanderer and His Shadow*.

#27: The "take or leave" binary refers to the ethical argument at the heart of Daniel Quinn's *Ishmael*.

#33: "Pillars" is used here in the strict sense of Jewish temple architecture—those framing the entrance to the Kodesh HaKodashim, where even the high priest could only enter once a year, for that was the seat of God. It is implied that the outer pillars *Boaz* (strength) and *Jachin* (to establish) are present in the poem as well, for how fitting it is that the purpose of these are still debated.

#43: For a thorough illustration of the provocative intimacy of architecture, both in format and content, see Mark Z. Danielewski's *House of Leaves*.

#45: The use of "space" vs. "names" here invokes a psychological interpretation of Plato's "forms" vs. material substance, wherein the disruption of the infinite by specifics generates fear and risks misrepresentation.

ABOUT THE AUTHOR

Jason David Peterson was born and raised in Minnesota. He received his Masters in English at the University of Wisconsin with an emphasis in creative writing, and currently cohosts the Saint Paul Poetry Workshop. His poetry has been recognized in the back alleys of literature with scholarships, nominations, and awards in Canada and the U.S.

www.ingramcontent.com/pod-product-compliance
Lightning Source LLC
Chambersburg PA
CBHW071734040426
42446CB00012B/2361